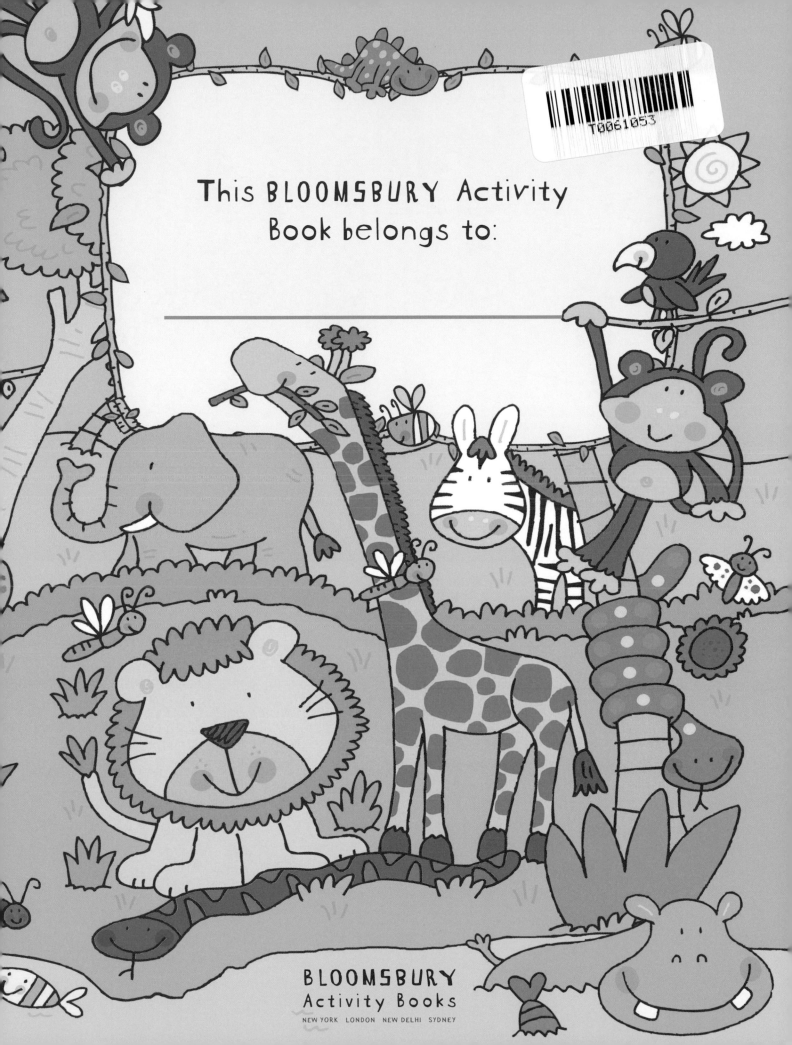

This BLOOMSBURY Activity
Book belongs to:

BLOOMSBURY
Activity Books
NEW YORK LONDON NEW DELHI SYDNEY

Spot the differences between the 2 elephant

pictures. There are 8 to find.

Color in Farmer Carter and Mrs. Carter.
They live on Bloomfield Farm with Holly
and Jim and a dog called Scamp.

Fill the page with
crow and snail stickers.

Color in Jim and Holly
in the farm shop.

8

9

Add duck stickers to the pond.

Can you spot the matching sheep?

Find some fish stickers
to add to the aquarium.

Color in Jim and
Mrs. Carter feeding
the chickens.

15

Color the patterns on the snakes.

16

Doodle more butterflies and snails.

Color the animals to match the opposite page.

Help the lost giraffes through the maze to reach their friends.

22

23

Draw some monkeys playing in the trees.

24

26

Color in Holly and Jim picking apples.

27

How many rabbits, guinea pigs, sheep,

and goats are in Pets' Corner?

Can you find the matching pairs?

31

Color in Farmer Carter's plow.

32

Doodle more fish to fill the page and color them in.

Write a story about an owl.

- -

- -

- -

- -

- -

- -

Draw the owl and his friends here.

Doodle spots and stripes
on the elephants.

Color in the farm show.

41

Draw more flowers, crows, and rabbits on this page.

Fill the pages with hens and color them in.

Can you count 9 purple feathers

46

on the parrots?

Color in the
garden picture.

48

49

Count all the cats in the big cat area

and add spider stickers to the page.

51

Spot the differences between the
2 pictures. There are 8 to find.

Color in the farmyard picture.

55

Add vegetable stickers to fill the garden.

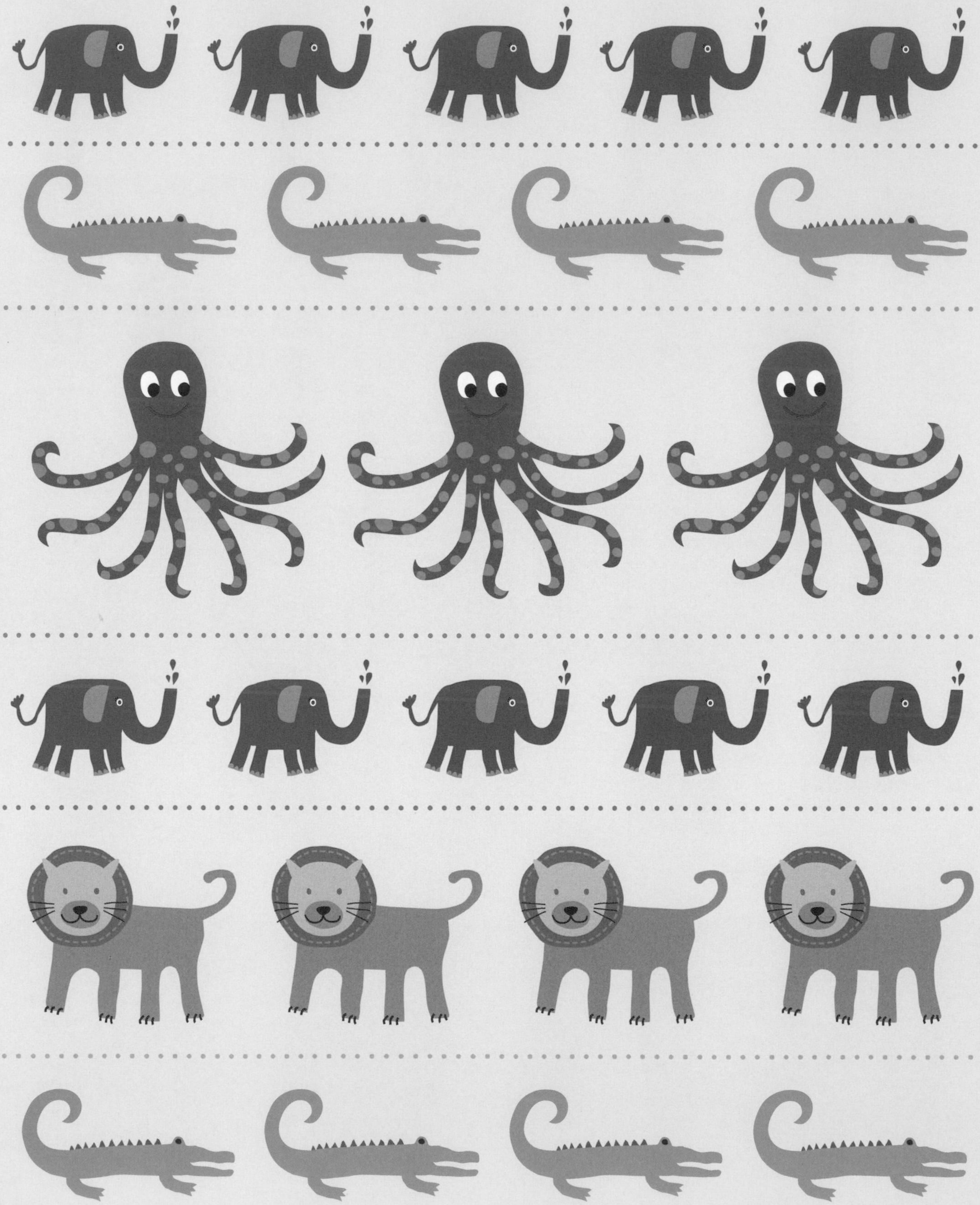

Color the animals to match the opposite page.

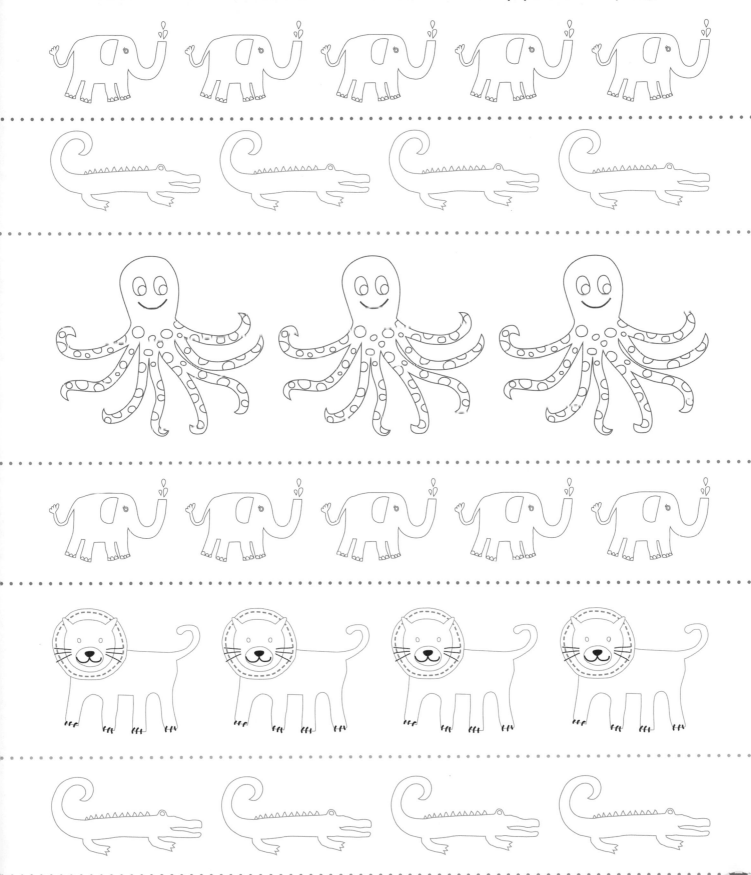

59

Doodle hats on all the penguins.

Add fish stickers to this page.

Color in this farmyard scene.

62

Can you spot the different one?

Color in the picture of sheep and a tractor.

Draw 3 dogs on the tractor.

Count the geese.

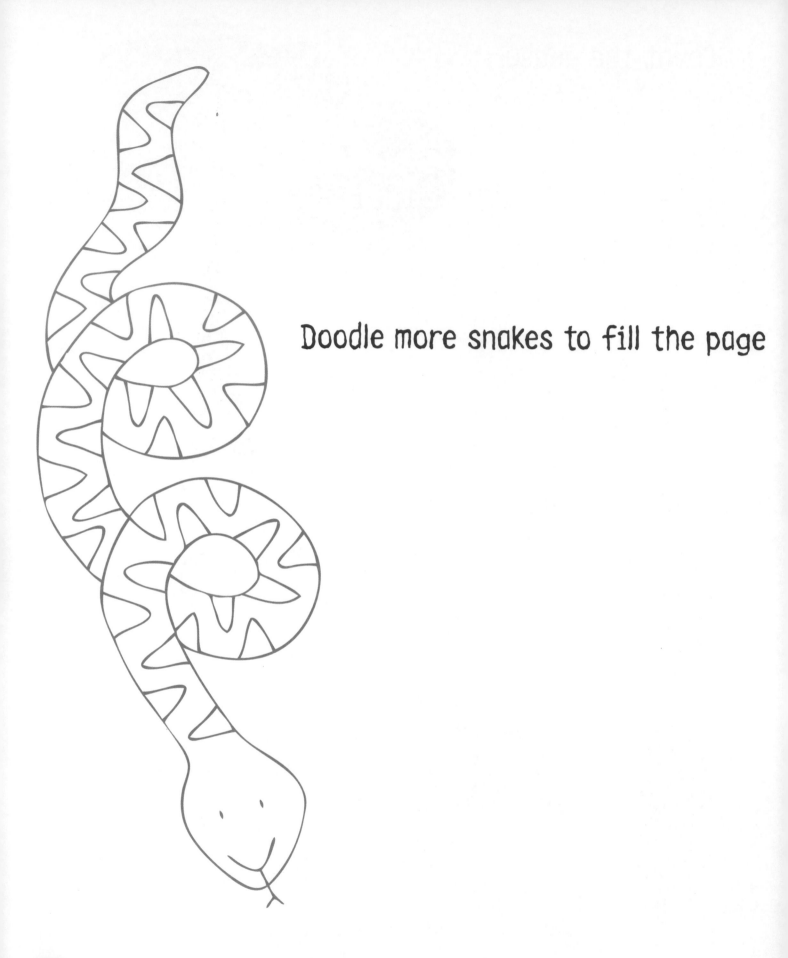

Doodle more snakes to fill the page

and color them in.

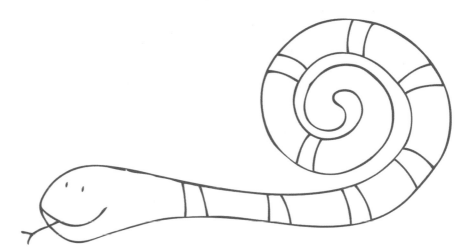

Fill the page with giraffes.

Color in the
farmhouse kitchen.

75

Add flower and hen stickers
to this picture.

76

Fill the page with more
insect and bird doodles.

Which balloon belongs to which meerkat?
Follow the strings to find out.

Color in the pigs
in the pigsty.

83

Write a story here about a cat.

Draw the cat and his friends here.

Doodle more pigs and sheep.
Color them in.

Search the picture and find 5 butterflies,

88

4 spiders, 3 beetles, 2 snails, and a toucan.

Color in Holly and Farmer Carter feeding the horses.

Draw a line between the matching

pairs in the reptile house.

Fill the pages with

cats and dogs and color them in.

Can you spot the panda?

97

Color in Jim and
Holly fishing in
the duck pond.

98

Spot the differences
between the 2 pictures.
There are 6 to find.

Write a story here about a horse.

....

....

....

....

....

....

Draw the horse and his friends here.

Color the animals to match the opposite page.

Draw a line to
match the shadows
to the animals.

Color in the picnic picture.

109

Color in the crocodiles.

Spot the mouse,
rabbit, puppy,
and kitten
hiding in the
scarecrow.

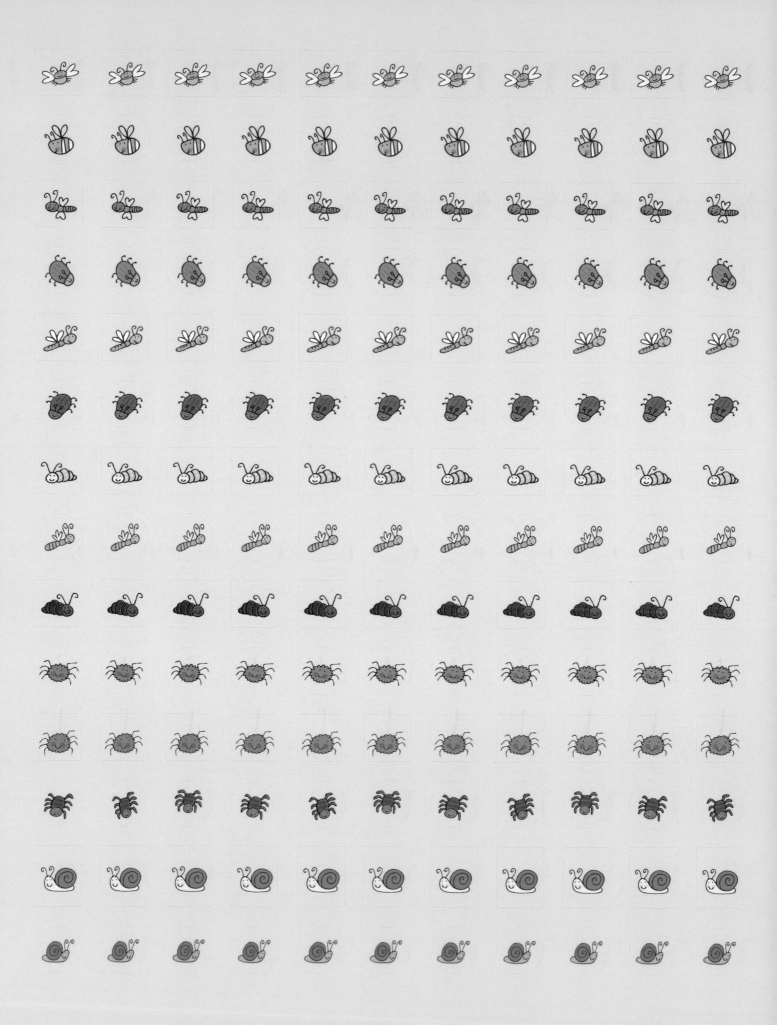

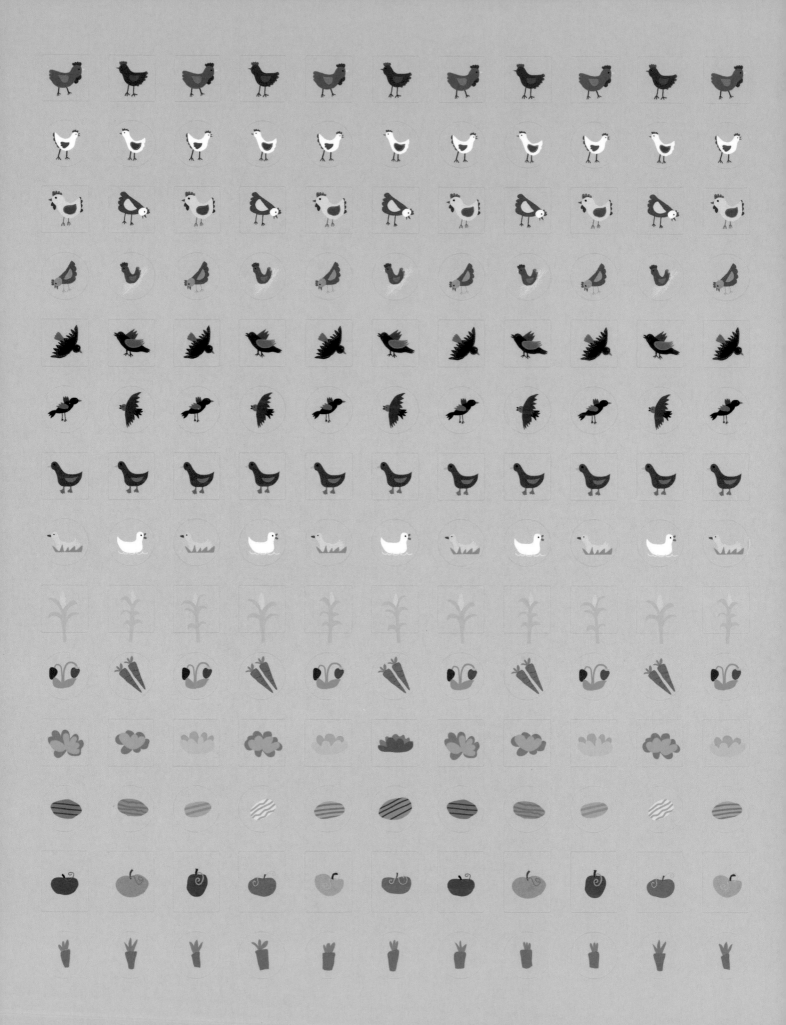

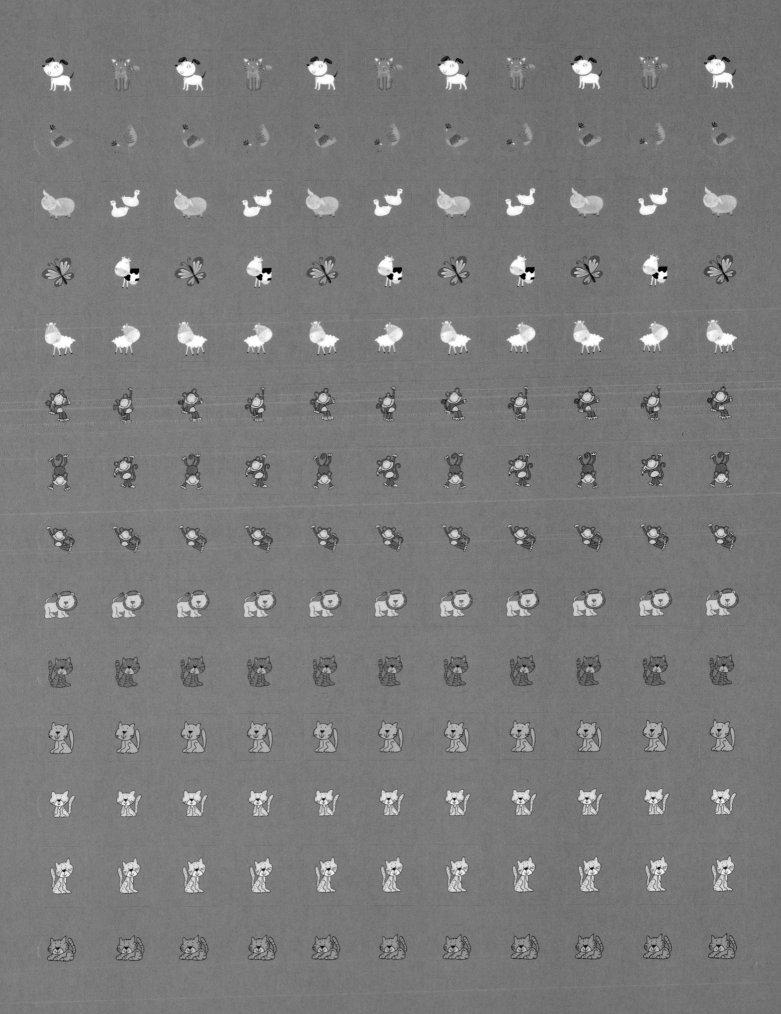

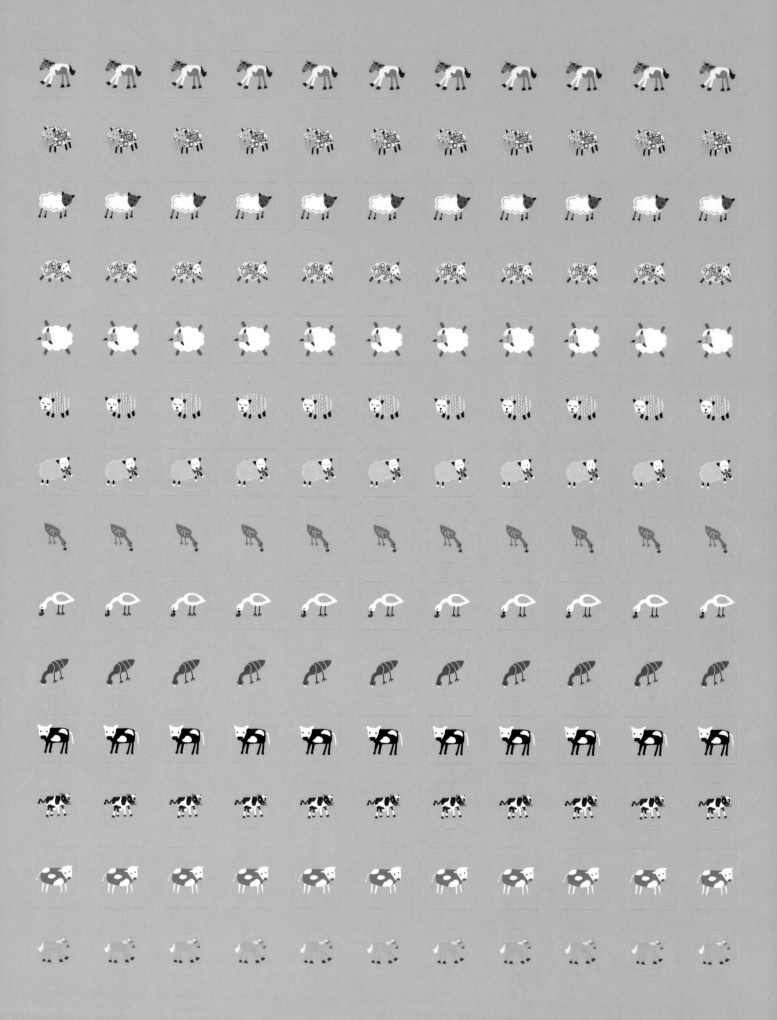